Horse Training

Foundational Principles Of Equine Training For Novices: Establishing Trust And Ensuring Compliance With Fundamental Commands

(Essential Information To Consider About Your Horse Prior To Commencing Training, Horse Training)

Sheldon McLellan

TABLE OF CONTENT

HORSE TRAINING METHOD - A TECHNIQUE TO REDUCE OBEDIENCE IN YOUR HORSE..1

Changing Foods...53

Extra Vitamins, Grain or Feed..................87

Section 5: The Methodologies............... 107

HORSE TRAINING METHOD - A TECHNIQUE TO REDUCE OBEDIENCE IN YOUR HORSE

Learning some horse training techniques is helpful if you want to train your horse to be obedient and easy to ride. Of course, a patient and well-trained horse makes for a perfect companion. A calm and receptive horse often exhibits these qualities.

You probably wish you could talk to your horse and tell him what to do, but because you cannot, you must teach him body language and commands so you may eventually get your horse to do what you want.

These are some of the most often used methods in dog training.

Quicker training

One of the horse training techniques you may use to get your horse to perform anything is clicker training. This training method uses a clicker that you can regularly purchase from a pet store. Additionally, you must have drills as backups for every command or skill your horse will pick up.

Although it was initially used to train marauding animals, clicker training is now also used for training horses. This type of training involves positive reinforcement and benefits the animal without injuring or forcing it to do what you want.

This training method typically begins with teaching your horse that a "short" horse is a trainee. You may teach him how to read and write by clicking and giving him practice problems. You can begin with basic commands and small skills, but ensure you give him his treat or incentive each time he performs well.

It isalsoimportanttoholdyourtrainingsession in shortperiodsof time tomakeyourclickertrainingeffective.

Ensure that you only return the appropriate behavior. Steer clear of the temptation to encourage inappropriate behavior, which can become more difficult to break.

Continuing

One of the often utilized horse training techniques is lunging. This involves using a long line that you can hold at a distance from the person. Thelongeline is aropefastenedtothe head of the horse while the trainer can teach him tolistento orders andallowthehorsetomove around the circle. This is typically performed in a large circle where you can stand in the center.

A good technique to teach your dog to listen to voice commands is healing, especially if you teach a young dog who is not yet accustomed to it. It will also enable the animal to learn how to respond to the trainer's body language and "read" it.

This method can also be applied if the horse cannot be ridden or if you would like to see an improvement in his gait and better balance and rhythm. To make your horse training as simple as possible, you might need to think about introducing additional equipment used during longeing.

Start using these two horse training techniques, and you and your horses will experience the benefits of a well-trained horse.

HÐRSж TRÑINING: TEACH YOURSELF FOUR LESSONS

Which four dog training lessons are the most crucial? Experts advise teaching your horse about motivation, direction, and recall.

As these lessons are essential to the training program, it doesn't matter if you're training a dog or a cat. As the herd leader, you must act and not allow your horse to control you.

In addition, horse training focuses on correct control. Building a brick house can be compared to training hours. It requires some time before you can finish developing it. Thus, you should take your time teaching your horse the many lessons in the training regimen. It should be simple to control the many parts of your horse's body; you can begin by controlling one section at a time. While doing this, you must act like a vibrant rider rather than a reactive one.

ENTHUSIASM

This is the first lesson to introduce yourself to your horse. In nature, horses are wild animals. They sleep, groom, eat, and play. However, they are also known as wild animals; some even operate their entire herd. You must take the lead in leading your horse to effectively train them. Since you will be training your horse, it will be as if you ask it to do your work. Consider what will encourage your equine to adhere to the training regimen you have established for him. You must acknowledge that horses do not desire to be led. However, it doesn't stop there. You shouldn't quit just yet.

S

Here's where ϵpot' comes in. Find a specific point you can control so your horse will follow. This could take some time, but it's just attempting to recognize the right position on the horse's body.

DIRÕáTIÞN

Once you've located a location, you need to choose the direction. The horse's body may move in all directions: left, right, forward, backward, below, and upward. Select just one direction. Ensure your horse understands your signals or assistance to avoid confusion.

AWARD

This concludes the lesson. When your horse follows your originals, remember to give him a gift. You have two options: give him a treat or give him a gentle pat and say, "That's a good boy/girl."

The four classes appear simple initially, but things change when you practice. Managing persistent headaches is difficult and will take a lot of patience. If you neglected to practice, don't hesitate to consult the experts. It is important to remember that not all employers are unsatisfactory; some are quite easy to work with. Teaching the four lessons one at a time is the key. You'll run into fewer issues when your horse knows the lessons.

Identifying an interacting factor is not as easy as you may imagine. Start early. Additionally, you should be a skilled driver so you won't have trouble deciphering the horse's movements. Find out everything you can about proper horse training. You must observe the behavior and personality of the horse. Try to figure out how to incorporate these four lessons into your training regimen. I hope this helps.

4 Never Put Your Safety First

Consistency is crucial when training a young horse.

I've always taken great satisfaction in training horses with the utmost consistency. For me, having perfect form and bending on a turn is crucial. My approach is to go slowly until a horse can follow the pattern consistently, and then I increase the speed.

"You don't have a very good horse if it can't make two runs in a day," my father would usually say.

Then he told me that they were not ready to run unless I could slowly walk my horses through the pattern without using my hands. He insisted on using leg cues when training a horse. He thought you could save their mouth by utilizing your feet instead of your hands because they were inconsistent. Before he declared we were ready to go faster, the first horse I trained made me place my hands on my head and trot her through the pattern.

I concur with my father. At least twice a day, your horse should be able to complete the same run. If you utilize leg cues instead of simply your hands to turn, your horse will turn more consistently. However, that does not imply that I have always had reliable horses. Some lacked the mental and physical stamina to run nonstop more than once in the afternoon. I put in considerably more effort with these horses to strive for excellence. I think I put a lot more effort and focus into them than I did the simple horses. Regretfully, despite my intense desire for excellence, I had to concede that many horses were simply unfit for the task.

I find horses and people to be quite similar. They have a mouth, a nose, two ears, and two eyes on a physical level. They may have a tail and extra legs but still have all the major organs, including the heart and lungs. They develop and learn in a similar way to how humans do. They must learn their ABCs when they are young. They can manage more challenging subjects as they age, such as learning to run barrels or rope. Similar to children, they can suffer physical and mental harm if they are pushed too hard at an early age. The same applies to horses—those extraordinary children always do incredible feats. People often struggle to recognize that horses, like people, are all unique regarding personality and character. They are not all the same regarding how they learn, become successful, or respond to others. Each of them is distinct and different.

I was lucky to have a father who supported me in my love of horses from a young age. When I was eight, I began riding my horse and would mount any animal. My dad found me work riding horses for other people as a teenager. It taught me so much about horses and strengthened my horsemanship talents. Being able to ride a variety of horses allowed me to develop as a horseperson.

That happened with a family friend who allowed me to train a horse on their behalf. Not simply any old pal or any kind of training, but a potential barrel horse for some well-known and fierce barrel racers!

Mr. Burton was wed and had two strong and gifted daughters who rodeoed. They were renowned for always placing and being difficult to beat. They roped, ran barrels, and tied goats.

Mr. Burton and his family handed me an eight-year-old gelding that appeared large and sorrel. He had a big head, yet he was quite fit and muscular. It was called a "jug head," which didn't match his svelte, athletic build.

"Cut his head off, and he's a good-looking horse," is what we all remarked, but the gelding was an athlete with outstanding genes and had the potential to be a good barrel horse. They offered me the opportunity to train him since they knew I could consistently train horses. I was incredibly touched and resolved to give it my all.

The gelding was deft at side passing and knew when to lead. He appeared composed and yielded to the pressure. He became proficient at interpreting my cues quickly and began using the pattern often.

The first barrel was the one issue that irritated me. When I picked up the speed, he could not produce a good first barrel. If I let him slow down, he would spin it incredibly tightly, but if he was running hard, it would go wide. I wanted the better turn, but he was losing too much time slowing down. I put much effort into helping him solve the first barrel problem daily. I searched my mind for alternative workouts to attempt and other things that could be useful.

We were running the pattern, and I was hauling him after approximately two months of training, but the first barrel remained problematic. I even ran him at one of my college rodeos since I didn't have a horse then. I had to make a split-second decision: do I run him hard and risk him going wide, or should I slow him down to make a good turn? I would have to spend time on both.

I chose to be cautious and reduced my speed.

Although our initial barrel rotation was successful, it took far too long.

I returned the horse to Mr. Burton and his family the next week. I felt sorry for myself. I felt like I had failed when I attempted to make an inconsistent horse consistent for the first time with this horse. "You never safe up at the race," Mrs. Burton retorted when I told her about our run at the college rodeo. She was correct, and I realized that I had chosen poorly. Even though I was young, I learned from my error. I never again used a safety pin!

5 The Nanny

"You mean he wasn't instructed?"

My dad answered, "We trained him on the barrels, but he was a heading and tripping horse."

Not because he was descended from the well-known racehorse Oklahoma Fuel, but rather because he was from Oklahoma; my first genuine horse was a large brown gelding named "Okey." We didn't purchase him in Oklahoma, which is a little confusing. My dad purchased him from a close friend who resided in our hometown. Mr. Moss was a highly renowned steer tripper and team roper. His residence was conveniently located near a busy highway, and he owned multiple quality horses. The pipe fence, fine barn, lit arena, and immaculately groomed meadows were proof of his prosperity in the growing oilfield. He also possessed a few nice horses, but he was ready to give my dad Okey in exchange for me getting my first horse.

I was eventually able to compete in the local 4-H horse events when I was eight years old. It was well known that our county produced some of the state's most difficult-timed and judged event riders. Presumably, because there were so many well-known, experienced professional horse trainers in our region who were willing to share their knowledge with local children as well as their own. The riders were extraordinarily skilled, and the horses were fiercely competitive during the 1980s oil boom. In district and state contests, our county performed exceptionally well. Many children I knew became professional horse trainers after success in collegiate competitions. I would finally get my chance to compete and learn from them.

Okey initiated me into the barrel racers' club, whose registered name was Rebel Master. Although he was a strong horse, everyone soon found that he was also one of the best nannies in the area. Though strong and swift, he would also look out for his youthful rider. My dad took me to the pasture next to our house the first time I loped him. He was riding a different horse next to me, and while encouraging me to send Okey galloping, he also galloped alongside me. I still use that analogy now when guiding inexperienced riders. He remarked, "Sit back like you are rocking in a chair." Okey was gentle with me and taught me how to trot, lope, and maintain control.

I learned to step on the fender of the horse trailer and throw my saddle above his back. Even though I was very short as an adult, It would sometimes land precisely, and other times, it would just fall to the ground. Even if Dad couldn't help, I would be able to saddle him. I did not know enough about caring for him and wanted to handle everything myself.

My dad started setting up the barrels when I was finally riding well. I would follow his instructions when he gave them to me. Growing up, my dad had ridden colts and barrel horses, so he knew that training required persistence and patience. Walk three, trot three, then lope three. That was the pattern repetition he had me perform. We would increase the speed after we were reliable.

I was afraid of the speed. I would cry and plead with my father to slow me down. When I was a little child, I allowed my fear to control me, but my dad was firm. I can't thank him enough for teaching me to face my concerns because he would force me to at least try to move faster. That's what made me such a formidable rival. Even as I become older, I still try to keep that boldness while teaching troublesome horses and riding young horses.

My dad didn't have an option back then, but he doesn't think it's a good idea to train the child and the horse together these days. Okey was a unicorn. I learned how to stay motionless and steer him in the appropriate direction, and he could take care of me. It required time. We took some time to triumph.

Indeed, one of my first major events was held just a short distance from our home. There was fierce rivalry and a large number of grownups. I was nervous. We ran a great run and might have even won, but I ran home on the wrong side of the second barrel. Okay, I was truly blinded by his dazzling speed! I wasn't even aware I had violated the pattern until I received a "no time" for it. Despite his anger, my father never gave up on me.

After some while, we started to pick up speed. By the time I was ten, we were placing or winning practically everywhere we went, even the 4-H horse events. I was outpacing grownups, even though I was only a young child. My dad knew what he was doing, but many others believed he had me on too much horse. Okey was powerful, fast, and all that, sure, but he was always our babysitter. The clearest illustration of this that I can think of is when my younger brother was riding Okey in the poles when he had finally reached the age at which he could compete in 4-H. Okey stopped in the middle of the pattern when his girth broke. Okey remained motionless like a statue until assistance came, while my brother and the saddle gradually fell off the side. He knew his rider all the time.

I will always remember the incredible runs we had. Now, I could never have imagined owning a horse like that. After thirty years of looking, I have not yet discovered a horse that mirrored Okey. He was the ideal starter horse I could have wished for and a meaningful part of my life.

As I grew older, my family utilized Okey for more than pole bending and barrel racing. He was also the one who taught my older brother how to rope. Regretfully, that proved to be his undoing. He bent a tendon. Back then, you had to let the horse go, but nowadays, there are many things we can do to aid with that kind of injury. My father sold him to a well-to-do family in town, who used him as their first horse for the children. They didn't fight over him. All they wanted to do, which was ideal for Okey, was learn how to bike. They cared for him and kept us informed about his progress.

I didn't discuss Okey with my dad until I was in my thirties. At that point, he revealed that the gelding with whom I had gone on incredible runs was not a trained barrel horse. All those years, I believed he was a finished horse, and I was the one getting my barrel-running skills together! As it turns out, my dad was training both of us simultaneously. You have no idea how surprised I was! I discovered that I had been training barrel horses since I was eight.

What do you think about that?

Everything About Equines Training Techniques

For every horse, different approaches will produce different outcomes. While some strategies emphasize a soft approach, others take a more aggressive stance. Naturally, the trainer has just as much influence on the chosen method as the horse has. Most handlers would rather employ soft methods than rough methods when training horses. Be aware that being kind does not mean being helpless.

Being gentle encourages the horse to trust your leadership.

The Method of Breaking

As was previously indicated, breaking entails coercing the horse into a subservient manner. Recently, this practice has become less common due to criticism that it is somewhat inhumane.

The Method of Joining Up

Monty Roberts created this method to facilitate natural communication between a handler and their equine companion. He also came up with the name 'Equus" the silent communication between horses. A trainer starts this procedure by putting a new horse in a pen. The horse will then be encouraged to run by the trainer's loud noises, which will mimic a threat. When this occurs, the trainer uses body language to force the horse to choose between backing away and joining in. It is deemed successful when the horse responds to this strategy by showing respect by lowering his head or locking an ear with its trainer.

The Method of Natural Horsemanship

This approach is more of a philosophy emphasizing teaching a horse via gentle encouragement. According to this concept, treating a horse this way is the greatest way to gain their respect. The trainer will subsequently reward the horse's good behavior. This approach fosters a close relationship and increases trust between the trainer and the horse.

The Method of Pleasure Horse Training

Show horses are also referred to as "pleasure horses." Horses undergoing this form of training must be handled strictly for them to learn complex commands. Only when a horse's trainer already has a good rapport with him and can confidently direct him can show training commence. A handler gives basic cues such as walk, lope, and trot to initiate this procedure. The trainer will next concentrate on managing the horse's speed after that. The key to this strategy is to keep the animal relaxed because performance will make the horse stressed and under a lot of pressure.

The Tricks To Training Horses

You may feel a little overwhelmed now that you realize there are numerous approaches to training your horse. But there are some tricks you can employ to advance from novice horse handling to expert level!

Strengthen Your Bond with Your Horse

Establishing a positive relationship with your horse and comprehending his characteristics is critical. Despite not being human, they each have a distinct personality type. You must ascertain whether your equine is well-mannered, shy, erratic, or overbearing. Maintaining a horse's focus is essential when working with him. Speak to him in a soothing, collected tone.

This book will cover a lot of ground, one of which is the importance of remembering to commend positive behavior. Because it fosters solid relationships and reinforces positive conduct, this is an extremely important activity that should be repeated.

Training sessions will be simpler if you and your horse continue to have a strong relationship.

Recognize your body language.

In the wild, horses are prey, as was previously established. This implies that they will always be aware of your body language and be vigilant. When you first approach your horse, approach from the front but from a diagonal position; this occurs because the eyes of a horse are situated on the sides of his head. Recognize the body language of your horse as well. The ideal condition is met when he displays a lowered head, relaxed tail, and calm gaze. When a horse displays these traits, he is alert and at ease.

Help Your Equine Overcome Fear

Removing anything that could cause your horse unnecessary stress until he has complete faith in you is essential. Try not to let dogs anywhere near him. Riding crops and whips aren't necessary for training and can make your horse run away from you out of fear, so avoid using them.

Taking the lead

It's critical to understand good horsemanship to facilitate future training. The ideal lead line material is soft rope. Grab one end of the rope with your right hand while standing beside your horse's left shoulder. Make sure the distance between your shoulder and your horsehorse is one foot. Keep him from slipping behind or ahead of you. Maintain a constant speed and watch that he doesn't cross the distance marker you've put with his feet. Push your horse's muzzle gently away if he approaches too closely until he returns to his rightful position.

Maintain Regularity in Your Training Sessions

It is ideal to start your training session when your horse is relaxed. This implies that he needs to eat and get plenty of sleep. The ideal weather for exercising in an arena or outdoors is when the temperature is right. Start every training session by warming up with your horse. Go with him for a brief walk. Gently pat your horse's sides and speak softly to boost his confidence. Remember that routines are crucial, so practice the same commands repeatedly until he masters them. Only as long as your horse is content and motivated to work should each session continue.

Additional Hints and Techniques

Being able to successfully train your horse is a fulfilling experience. As you develop your relationship with your horse, learning new skills and maintaining your confidence and knowledge can help you make excellent progress. Your horse will become very knowledgeable and self-assured very soon.

Positive encouragement

Using prizes or carrots to train your horse is known as "positive reinforcement," whereas using sticks is known as "control." Positive reinforcement is giving the horse instructions to perform a task, such as accelerating or decelerating, then rewarding him with a carrot or other delectable treat when he succeeds. It will take some time to persuade the horse to speed or slow down precisely because it may not know how much to do.

Making it extremely tough for the horse to do the incorrect action while making the proper one very easy is one-way trainers make sure they can apply positive reinforcement.

It's crucial to remember that your horse shouldn't be giddy with anticipation for the rewards. If you take this too far, your horse may become unmotivated to work until he receives a treat. Avoid doing this as much as you can because it is a type of misconduct. Performing the command is the aim before rewarding him with a treat.

In charge

Teaching your horse that you are in charge is part of this training technique. They are unaware that horses are bigger and stronger than people. A common manipulation technique is known as "doubling." You must pull the horse's head back where you wish it to turn. A tiny kick should encourage the horse to advance when he obeys that command. You should perform this trick three or four times in a session when riding an untrained horse.

Clicker Instruction

We shall go into more detail regarding this common take on "positive reinforcement" in the upcoming chapter. When a trainer utilizes a signal as a reward rather than a goodie, it's called clicker training. When your horse obeys an instruction, but you cannot give them a treat, this strategy has an advantage. A horse can link a positive outcome with the clicking sound through clicker training. For instance, there's a delicious treat to go along with the clicking sound. The trainer will only use the clicker to reward the horse once it has established a bond.

Maintaining consistency is essential.

If you employ a certain strategy, do it as frequently as possible. Ideally, you could dedicate multiple days a week to horse training and riding. Your horse will trust and understand you more when you spend together. Similarly, that time with your horse will help you understand him more.

Basics of Clicker Training

Some zoos still employ this technique, originally used to train marine animals. This enables a trainer to identify desired behavior and subsequently reward it through the use of positive reinforcement. In this manner, your horse won't have to pick up multiple incorrect behaviors before learning the correct one by habit. All the other bad actions go unnoticed when he is rewarded for doing so morally. This kind of strategy makes eager pupils out of horses, and they learn lessons quickly.

Clicker training works well, whether on the saddle or from the ground. Basic ground manners and even advanced dressage maneuvers can be taught with this training. It's an excellent approach to supplement other training methods; all you need to know to use it with other techniques is the fundamentals.

You'll need the following before you start clicker training:

A clicker. This is available online or in pet retailers.

A sack or container to keep prizes. Most trainers utilize fanny packs.

Candy! Ensure you have tiny bits of your horse's favorite reward. Carrot slices, sugar cubes, apple cubes, horse crunch, and mints are a few examples.

Teaching your horse to wait for a treat when he hears the click is the first thing you need to do. The horse is typically taught this by keeping it in a box stall with the trainer standing on the opposite side of a closed door. You just click to reward him with a treat. After about ten repetitions of this, release him. After 30 minutes, carry out the same procedure. Before the horse comprehends, you must go through this entire process greatly. Although it's common to anticipate that a horse would require a few extra sessions, occasionally, a horse will get things up quickly.

Make your sessions brief!

It is crucial to keep in mind this advice. Less than five to ten minutes should elapse between each clicking and treatment session. Several brief sessions are more productive than one lengthy one. It's simple to get carried away, particularly when a horse is incredibly excited, but remember to keep an eye on the clock!

Focused Instruction

Teaching horses to touch a target is another approach to start clicker training. Take your horse to his stall and practice working over the door. A target will also be necessary. Use your creativity and grab something easy to see and grasp, such as an empty shampoo bottle or a plastic plate.

Raise the target and position it to face your horse's nose. Verify that he can see it. With horses' innate curiosity, he'll likely bump it with his nose when it comes to target training; time matters! Use the clicker as soon as your horse bumps against the target. Present a treat right away following. Once more, place the target in front of your horse. Click and treat it every time he bumps it.

You can click and treat each time your horse looks at the goal if he doesn't feel like touching it alone. Even a slight bob in the target's direction is considered. Remember to be patient and encourage your horse's little steps. Once more, remember to work in short bursts.

Teaching your horse to follow the goal is the next phase. Hold the target down or off to the side rather than in front of him. The horse will soon pick up the skill of trailing the target into a stall. It can also be used to make the horse remain motionless while it is being groomed and untied. With clicker and target training, it can take many more helpful actions!

Steer clear of these errors.

Positive reinforcement training always carries the risk of unintentionally rewarding erroneous conduct. Some horses become restless for their reward because they are so fond of the gift you are offering. Do not click or give treats to a horse that paws you to receive them.

Treating a horse too soon is another mistake you can make because it makes the animal demanding of goodies. However, you can distribute rewards at your own pace after you click. You can adjust the timing of the click, which signals the horse that a treat is on the way.

Changing Foods

It can eventually become evident that, for various reasons, switching to hay or grain is necessary. Use this switching schedule to swap out brands or types of food:

Day 1–2 Blend ¼ new and ¾ old meals.

Days 2-4 Combine ½ new and ½ old.

Days 5 and 6 Combine ¾ new and ¼ old.

Day 7: All new food, 100%

As mentioned above, you should begin gradually when transitioning your Friesian horse, for example, from Alfalfa to Orchard Grass Hay. Because Alfalfa contains more protein than other grass hay, you might discover that your

Friesian horse is getting overweight. It would be wise to test him on Orchard Grass or another type of grass hay. You'll probably notice that his conduct has improved. You could use "Mare Magic" on your Friesian mare to balance her mood based on her cycles. Her behavior will probably improve, and you will notice it. Mare Magic can likewise improve a Gelding's mood. You might cut back on your Friesian horse's feed after noticing he has too much fat around his ribs.

To help your Friesian horse gain weight again, you can decide to add some rice bran to his diet after seeing that you can feel or see his ribs. It is typical to alter or modify your Friesian horse's diet to preserve optimum health. You are advised to contact your veterinarian if you are unsure.

Healthy Snacks and Treats

You can include the following nutritious human meals in your Friesian horse's diet or give him as treats:

A delight of oats and molasses

Oatmeal and apple snacks

Pears and Apples

Different treats for horses from your feed store

Pumpkin or squash

Carapace

How to Work Out Your Friesian Horse

The health of your Friesian horse depends on exercise. Friesian horses require exercise to keep healthy, just like people do. As they age, inactive Friesian horses are more likely to develop obesity and cardiac, joint, and muscular problems. Furthermore, a bored Friesian horse can become unruly due to a lack of activity. Providing your Friesian horse with plenty of exercise and unstructured outside activities in his pasture is important.

Friesian horses need to exercise for thirty minutes to two hours every day. Friesian horses require two hours or more of exercise and pasture time daily. You may give him some of this exercise by letting him run around in his pasture.

You need to be proactive about some of these activities. When he has finished his feed in the morning, go into his paddock, put on his halter using the lead line, and tie him (leaving some slack) to the hitching rail.

Get out his brushes and brush his whole body completely. Remove all the tangles by brushing his mane and tail. The second and third days won't have many tangles if you regularly brush your Friesian horse's mane and tail. After cleaning your Friesian horse, put on his blanket and saddle if you plan to ride him for the day's exercise.

Giving your Friesian horse a thorough brushing each time is crucial before putting on the saddle. Make sure you brush out any burrs, foxtails, and dirt. You will not have a happy Friesian horse if you saddle him with a burr between his skin and his saddle. We advise taking lessons before you ride your Friesian horse if this is your first horse and you have never done so. Additionally, you can learn how to bridle and saddle your Friesian horse. You can put on his harness after adjusting the cinch of his saddle. Fasten his reins to the saddle horn (in the case of a western saddle) or, in the case of an English saddle, around the base of his neck close to the saddle. If you have a round enclosure, attach his long lead rope and take him to the middle of an empty pasture.

You can exercise your Friesian horse by having him walk, trot, or canter in circles around you to warm up his muscles. We will talk more about particular exercise training later. As a general guideline, perform ten canters, ten trots, and ten circles to walk to the left. Walk, trot, and canter to the right, then reverse course and repeat. He will be warm enough to ride after this. Additionally, it will help him release some of his stored energy, improving his behavior when riding after.

You're prepared to ride now. You could employ a mounting block to minimize lifting your leg high enough for your stirrups. Still, you must be able to mount in both directions. Introduce him gently. Ride him for 10-15 minutes the first time. The following day, try 15-20, then 20–25, and so on, following the same pattern until you reach one hour a day. As long as you are riding in an indoor ring, nothing should go wrong. Your Friesian horse could get fearful of leaving the stable if you are heading out to ride on a trail.

You might need to make a few shorter outings when leaving the stables first. You're less likely to run into issues if you begin riding your Friesian horse within a week of bringing it to the stables. A condition known as "barn sour" may cause your Friesian horse to become more fearful if you wait more than a week. This indicates that your

Friesian horse fears venturing outside his secure stables and into the wild or larger world.

The Friesian horse is an animal of prey. They are inherently afraid of being eaten by bears or cougars, and they never know what to do if they spot an elk or deer. If you encounter an unusual creature while hiking, prepare for your Friesian horse's anticipated reaction. You could be at risk from this. Your Friesian horse can attempt to toss you off his back or make such a long, quick jump that you just tumble off. I'm only trying to get you ready, not to frighten you. Certain Friesian horses will just stop and evaluate the circumstances. The most desired response is that one.

If your Friesian horse freezes and looks around, gently turn him away from the threat and walk him in that direction. Keep him from backing away from predators, not even at a trot. The bear or cougar will typically follow the running instinctively. Keep your Friesian horse at a trot; never run. Others will sprint in the other direction, and you could find it hard to keep him under control. It could be necessary for you to leap off or just hold on for a few hundred yards.

While you are building a relationship with your Friesian horse, there are a lot of problems you can have to deal with. You have to get ready ahead of time. He might turn out to be your true love. You ought to be aware of the risks and make preparations beforehand. When riding, we advise you to always use a safety helmet. If you are riding a trail, we advise you to go with a second rider whenever feasible. You'll get out and move more due to this physical activity. Simply put, saying.

Cleaning: Scrubbing

You should brush your Friesian horse's coat and clean his hooves at least four times weekly. Daily brushing is recommended when a Friesian horse starts shedding in the spring. Before the warm summer arrives, he will have to lose his whole winter coat.

It's mutually soothing, I can guarantee you, before the long day starts.

You and your Friesian horse will enjoy some of the most healing and uplifting moments together throughout this. As much as you enjoy brushing him, he will adore being brushed. While you are brushing him, converse with him. Talk to him frequently using his name. Say "good boy" each time he stands up straight. Say "Stand" if he starts to try to get away from you or move about. Say "Good Boy" to him when he stops moving, and then say it repeatedly. When they are young, some Friesian horses may try to bite or kick you. NEVER ALLOW EITHER TO OCCUR! You must take precautions for your safety whenever you are near your Friesian horse. Ensure he's not about to kick you by keeping a close eye on him. He might be considering it if he is standing with one leg bent back. If you never let him, he will never bite or kick you.

You might want to give him some room while you move around him to ensure that he misses his kick if he attempts. You have to smack his nose away and tell him, "No biting," if he attempts to chew on your arm. You only need to backhand lightly. If you do hit your Friesian horse, never hit it extremely hard. He will never consider biting or kicking you until he fully bonds with you. Brush his entire body, neck, face, and legs if necessary. You'll clean every inch of his body, from the muck to the dust.

Always take precautions to keep yourself safe. Brush his mane and forlock with a detangling brush, carefully brushing out all tangles. Feathers surround the hooves and lower legs of Friesian horses. For them as well, you should use a detangling brush. Some tangles require cutting out because they are so severe. Once the mane is done, do the same with his legs and tail. Maybe you can stand behind him and brush his tail in the future.

We advise you to start by standing to one side of his back and softly brushing his tail to one side. Remember that you and your Friesian horse may bond immediately or slowly. When selecting a Friesian horse, it is ideal for everyone if he feels lovable to you before purchase. That will guarantee that the bonding process happens considerably faster. The bonding process involves everything you do initially with your Friesian horse. With your Friesian horse, you are building a partnership that will last a lifetime of good health and happiness. Please savor every moment as you go.

Bathing Your new best friend might entice you to do so frequently. But remember that his natural oils keep his skin and hair healthy. Washing too much can remove those oils. As a result, it is recommended that you bathe your Friesian horse just once a season during the warm months. Use a warm water washing stall and get a high-quality horse shampoo, such as Mane & Tail Shampoo. For his tail and mane, the same brand of conditioner is offered.

1. Entice your Friesian horse to enter the laundry area.

2. Attach the lead rope of your Friesian horse to the hitching rail with care.

3. turn on the water after your Friesian horse is in the washing stall. Use your fingers to feel the water's temperature before immersing your Friesian horse. Make sure the water is lukewarm and pleasant.

4. After thoroughly wetting your Friesian horse's body, massage the shampoo to produce a light lather. Take care not to use so little that you can't get a rich lather or so much that you can't rinse it all out. Try your best to avoid his eyes and mouth. Rinse face when bathing if needed.

5. Tip: Give his head the last wash. This is the bit he would find objectionable.

6. Now rinse him well using lukewarm water.

Using your hands, gently massage the shampoo from top to bottom. Repeat this a few times to remove all of the shampoo so that his natural oils can start working to keep him healthy.

7. Now shut off the water and use a towel to pat him dry. Give him a good massage. Take him to a place where he can dry off in the sun. Remember that right after getting bathed, he will roll in the mud or dirt as soon as possible. It is best to wait until he is dry before allowing that.

paws

For gaiting and running, your Friesian horse needs his hooves to grip. You should polish your hooves when you bring your Friesian horse out of his stall. You would have been taught how to remove debris from the hooves, like manure and dirt, using a hoof pick during your training. It is crucial because tiny gravel fragments can become lodged and harm your Friesian horse. Cleanse each hoof by picking up each foot separately.

The majority of Friesian horses require hoof trims every six to eight weeks. You may hire a farrier to come and trim for you or learn how to do this with a trimmer and file. The trimmer resembles a hybrid of a nail clipper and a set of enormous pliers. The rough file is huge. Most of the time, the hoof can be filed smoothly in a few strokes after reducing it to a ¼ to ½ inch. Avoid cutting the hoof too short, as this may cause bleeding. After clipping, some owners always put shoes on their Friesian horses.

Some Friesian horses can walk anywhere without shoes because of their extremely strong hooves. Some people find it difficult to walk on jagged pebbles or stones. Strap-on shoes are an additional choice. These can be taken off when not needed and put on when needed. You may choose to wear shoes exclusively on your front two feet. This is usually sufficient since a Friesian horse typically places most of his weight on his front foot.

At the very least, you should have your Friesian horse trimmed by a farrier the first time. Should you want to trim yourself in the future, please take great care with the trimming. Costly are farriers. "You need to start with a large fortune if you want to have a small fortune after owning horses for a few years," it is said. Another proverb goes, "The human brain is the most amazing organ in the human body; it thinks and functions well every day, 365 days a year, from the moment of your birth until you fall in love with a horse." Thus, you might use this as a warning about the lifetime costs of owning a Friesian horse.

As you read this book, we anticipate it will already be too late. Either your current Friesian horse or the thought of getting your first One has already won your heart. In any case, it's probably too late to heed any caution. As I've already indicated, Friesian horses can be dangerous. It is estimated that 100 deaths annually in the United States result from riding or handling horses; most of these deaths are accidental, and the Friesian horse did not intend to kill the victim. An estimated 1000–2000 head injuries occur annually, most of which are treated with survival but leave the victim permanently altered. Again, for this reason, we advise you to use a safety helmet when riding.

The Teeth of Your Horse

Horses have teeth designed for grazing.

There are 12 incisors in the front of the mouth of an adult horse.

The premolars and molars are two of the 24 teeth designed for chewing.

"Tushes" are the extra four canine teeth stallions and geldings beneath their incisors.

In front of the molars, some horses—male and female alike—will also acquire one to four tiny vestigial teeth, or "wolf," teeth.

A horse's teeth can be used to determine how old it is.

Throughout life, teeth erupt and become worn down from grazing.

Horses experience variations in the angle at which the chewing surfaces touch, as well as a characteristic wear pattern and tooth form.

Horses' food digestibility is hampered if their teeth lack a flat surface to chew.

Regular dental examinations are a good idea, but no more than once a year is recommended.

Most veterinarians will advise having your horse's teeth floated every one to four years, but by the time your horse is ten, you should probably have floated your teeth. This involves filing your horse's sharp edges and points flat to provide a uniform chewing surface.

Eyes: Of all land mammals, horses have the largest eyes.

Horses can see over 350 degrees and have great day and night vision.

Similar to red-green color blindness in humans, horses have partial color blindness.

Your veterinarian should examine your Friesian horse's eyes regularly. Every day, you should examine the eyes of your Friesian horse. Regular inspection of his stall and paddock is necessary to remove any sharp or pointed objects, such as loose nails or screw tips poking through.

Additionally, search for and remove any loose, sharp wires or splinters. The reason is that there's a chance one of your Friesian horse's eyes will get punctured. During routine inspections, you might discover that one of your Friesian horse's eyes is almost swollen shut.

It's likely that your Friesian horse merely had a small piece of grass, dust, or grit lodged in his eye. Try using a medicine called "Vetericyn" Ophthalmic Gel for irritated eyes before calling the veterinarian. After cleaning your hands, apply a thick gel layer to your fingertip and place it slightly above his lower eyelid. He'll undoubtedly want to move away from you but resist the urge to let him touch your hand with his eye. His eye is itching and feels wonderful, so he'll want to do that. This will assist in distributing the gel across his eyeball's surface.

Should the edema not subside within a day, you can choose to schedule a stable appointment with your veterinarian. Even after losing one eye to blindness, some horses can still be ridden and function normally most of the time. Some horses go blind, but if there's no possibility of a stumble, they could be able to be ridden in mild terrain. That would only happen in a lifetime partnership between a strong horse and rider. This book is meant to educate you on how to create, tend to, and grow that lifetime relationship.

The lifespan of a horse is estimated to be 25 to 35 years. Some Horses survive into their forties and sometimes even older. In the 1800s, a horse was reported to have lived for 62 years. A pony is known to have died in 2007 at age 56.

Your friendship and affection with your Friesian horse will deepen with each passing year, even if most of it will blossom in the first year. I used to enjoy hugging my horse around the base of his neck, pressing my face against it to smell him, and pressing my chest against him. I used to do this with him before I bought him to make sure he was a docile horse with whom I could develop a bond.

HOW TO BODY CLIP A HORSE FOR WINTER IN CHAPTER 9

During the winter, body clipping your horse is a must. Wintertime coat growth can make a horse uncomfortable and hot and make it difficult to cool down.

As I mentioned in the last chapter, a good method to help your horse become less anxious and more at ease with clippers is to introduce them gradually. To help the horse get used to the sensation of the clippers, try stroking them against its body while they are off. You can lessen the likelihood that your horse will be spooked by the noise by turning on the clippers while it is far from them. You can talk to your horse to create a relaxed atmosphere during clipping.

Make sure to clip your horse's head and neck against the direction that the hair grows. Exercise caution when trimming the horse's feet and hindquarters because a startled horse can bolt. After cutting your horse, use a brush to remove extra hair. Make careful use of blankets to keep your horse warm after cutting.

Five Best Clipping Hints

Proceed cautiously with every step. Getting a horse used to the clipper might be difficult, so you should set aside as much time as you can the first time you do it. Before trimming, try to make sure the horse is in a relaxed mood. Preclipping care, including combing away matted hair, will help ease the horse's tension.

Choose a suitable time to expose a horse to clippers after you have groomed them for a short period. The process should be staggered; start the clippers safely from the horse but close enough to be audible. Assess your horse's response: does it appear frightened? If so, gently touch your horse and gradually approach the clippers while giving it some treats. You can proceed to the next level when the horse appears at ease.

If the horse exhibits resistance, back off and gently rub the clippers against its body. The horse may kick out if you approach with the clippers from the back. With your free hand, stroke the horse to release tension as you run the clippers over his body and back.

Start the clipping process, but be cautious—even if the horse appears at ease, one misstep might ruin the entire thing. It is advisable to concentrate on a complete clip at a later time and try to avoid clipping any delicate body parts the first time.

After trimming the horse, expressing your appreciation for good behavior—especially for timid horses- is critical to progress toward your goals. When the procedure is finished, praise the horse for being calm by giving him or her a few of their favorite goodies and displaying apparent affection.

Chapter 4: Maintaining Your Equines

Crucial Maintenance for Your New Horse

It's far easier to prevent future health issues for your horse if you start learning to care for him before bringing him home. Correct nutrition, care, and exercise are necessary for your horse to reach every stage of his life. Before bringing him home, you should have a veterinarian checkup. Oh, and be advised that he will likely resist or show signs of dread on your first visit. He will rapidly become friendly with the veterinarian and build trust before further visits. Keeping him cognitively and physically engaged throughout his life will reduce problem behaviors.

Consuming

The nutrition of your horse is crucial to its overall health. His age, degree of exercise, and breed will all influence his dietary requirements. Make sure you choose the right meal for his health. Here are some tips for feeding your horse and suggestions for the kinds of feed to use.

Dehydrated Animal Feed

Be sure to prioritize past feedings by the previous owner when selecting dry food. Alfalfa is preferred over grass hay by many horse owners. Legumes like lucerne are higher in protein than grass hay. If horses consume so much protein, some become "jacked up." Pay carefully if your horse seems more lively or shows behavioral issues. Try grass hay, like Timothy Hay or Orchard Grass, for a week if you observe this behavior and see if it stops. You should convert your horse to a grass hay diet if you discover that the lucerne is making them hyperbolic.

Extra Vitamins, Grain or Feed

Pick a horse food with a wide variety of vitamins and minerals. Supplements have been developed for all horses, including young, elderly, fat, and athletic horses. Super Supplement LMF - G is a vitamin supplement feed that I prefer to use. G is an acronym for grass hay. If you are giving your horse lucerne, you must get another variety. A quarter of a pound of LMF-G is given to my horses each morning and evening. Additionally, they are given one pound of COB twice daily, a blend of maize, oats, and barley. Due to recent weight loss, my eldest senior Horse is fed an additional ½ pound of rice bran twice a day to assist her in putting on weight.

Following their morning meal, the horses are released into the pasture during the dry seasons. For the most of the day, they can graze on the grass. They can eat almost a pound of grass in a single hour. Ensure every Horse has extra hay overnight if allowed to graze for ten hours. Most horses weigh about

1000 pounds, with the shoulder and greatest point of the body measuring 15 hands. This big Horse needs 20 pounds of hay per day in addition to pasture. Give your Horse an extra 10 pounds of hay in the evening for the night on days when it's believed that he grazed 10 pounds of grass.

You may keep your Horse inside the paddock on certain days due to inclement weather. You must provide each Horse with about 20 pounds of hay in their stall on those days. The grass has a very high sugar content in the early spring. Most horses should only spend a brief period in the pasture in the spring when new growth is expected. There is a second new growth season in the autumn in some years and locations. Because every nation's region is unique, pay attention to where you live.

This restriction on lush, fast-growing grass is due to the risk of overfeeding your Horse with sugar, which can cause them to "founder," leading to laminitis developing quickly. Your Horse may become severely crippled or perhaps die from laminitis. Limiting pasture time at these times of fresh grass growth is a safer way to prevent disease.

Wet Cuisine

For an old and toothless horse, a wet horse food diet may be helpful. If a horse cannot chew its hay, it can be replaced with soaked hay pellets. To prolong your Horse's life, feed it soaking pellets even if it hasn't had teeth in years. Typically, your Horse may begin to lose teeth at 25. They might not need to transition to a wet diet for at least five years.

Diet of Fresh Foods

Your Horse may benefit greatly from a fresh food diet because it more closely resembles what he would consume in the wild. However, if he is fed only grass, you must be careful not to let him get fired. Many horses can survive without extra hay, food, or vitamins. Plenty of horses can live in pasture year-round without ever getting laminitis. Your Horse needs constant access to FRESH and clean water if kept as a grazing animal. We would advise installing an automated irrigation system.

How Much Your Horse Should Be Fed

Your Horse's nutritional needs are determined by size, age, activity level, and endurance. If you can feel your Horse's ribs, you can determine if he needs extra food. You can tell if you feed him enough if his ribs are not showing through. You will need to reduce his feed if he starts to get fat on his ribs. A basic rule of thumb for hay or grass is to feed 2% of the Horse's body weight daily. This is predicated on the projected quantity of nighttime hay and/or pasture grass.

Remember that this is only a general guideline you can modify as necessary. However, remember that a mature horse weighs approximately 1000 pounds, so you should feed him about 20 pounds of grass or hay daily.

Starting to Move Forward Freely, Balance, and Suppling

Your First Assignment in the Arena

We will presume that the young Horse in training lunges well gets used to the mounting/dismounting, and walks and trots under the rider's weight. Physical strain will occur since the Horse's back, neck, and abdominal muscles are still weak and unaccustomed to bearing a rider. This tension will progressively subside as the muscles grow with appropriate exercise. However, new surroundings and a work regimen can also induce stress for a young horse and the rider's unfamiliar weight. A horse has to be emotionally and mentally at ease for his body to be free of tension. You, the rider, must be at ease for your Horse to relax. Before you can educate your Horse to operate in the same manner, you must teach yourself to be calm in both your body and head and ride your probable new animal relaxedly.

Exercise sessions should begin with a walk on a loose rein. Lunging a young horse before ridden work may calm him down if he is too enthusiastic, nervous, or new to the field for a walk on a loose rein. If lungeing is not an option, ride him gently in a rising trot while using the verbal cues he should be familiar with from his lunge training to calm and control him. Riding on curved tracks instead of straight ones helps a fidgety horse settle down more easily. Giving him easy activities to complete, like big circles or rein changes, will help divert his attention from the fascinating environment around him and help him focus on you. It can be quite challenging to calm a horse, especially an elderly one. You need to exercise patience because losing your cool will worsen the situation.

A stroll with a slack rein

Often, moving forward is the last thing on the mind of a freshly "broken" horse. Then, you will need to ride him strongly because once you get him moving, he can start to weave around and not know where to go. You must always firmly reassure your young Horse that he can trust you and that anything he is asked to do or go will be completely safe. In the early phases of training, napping or significant hanging back may occur if he is misinterpreted and treated too harshly or leniently. He must have the ability to always look forward and respond to the leg.

During this training phase, use a long rein to help the Horse become more adept at using its back correctly.

The meaning of the leg aids must be explicitly conveyed to the Young Horse. He learned to react to the lunge-whip and verbal cues from his lunge training. Now, he has to figure out what the rider's legs on his sides are trying to tell him. It is necessary to introduce the leg aids delicately. At this point, the voice must be used with the leg to help the horse understand that the leg means moving ahead or slowing down, depending on the aid utilized. A juvenile horse requires a lot of work because, in addition to not understanding the meaning of the rider's leg aids, he has no special motivation to travel. He finds it insignificant to go through a school, and he doesn't see the need to cut corners when it is much simpler and faster to go around them. You need to ride with strength, patience, and time to explain to the Horse why you want him to do this.

It may be easier to ride a young horse that is overly eager and sensitive to the leg at first, but in the end, he is likely to be a challenging, highly-strung horse with a disposition that is far from easy. By reducing the area of the arena in which you work with him, you can curtail the range of his emotions and avoid having to continually intervene with him in the future.

Once a horse learns to identify the leg aid with the vocal command, the leg aid can subtly increase as the Horse becomes more responsive, and the verbal aids can be gradually phased away. Teaching these early lessons to young horses is immensely satisfying. If the instruction has been done correctly, you should have less trouble later on with transitions, whether uphill or downhill.

An assistant in the middle of the arena can initially assist the very green Horse by holding a lunge-whip and utilizing his voice. With voice association, the green Horse will quickly be able to identify which leg assistance is whose.

During the first few weeks of basic training, you should teach the young Horse to help him move forward easily, find balance beneath the rider, and become more flexible.

Before putting the Horse through any more severe demands, going forward freely and balancing under the rider's weight must be well-established. He should step forward in front of your leg calmly, willingly, and freely. Never try to "put your horse on the bit." Continue riding forward without stopping to avoid "collecting" the Horse from the front. And don't mistake forward with impulsion. To build impulsion later on, you must move forward.

During the first few weeks of a young horse's schooling, putting him in a sitting trot or asking him to canter is inappropriate. You should only ride at a working canter pace, on a long rein, and in a light seat when the canter is introduced. When mature enough, a juvenile horse can only round his back and build the muscles necessary to canter in balance at a calm and leisurely pace.

When training a young horse, you should begin with a warm-up and loosening phase that lasts 15 to 20 minutes to prepare your Horse for work. You can lunge your Horse, take a quick hack, or walk him in the arena on a loose rein. After introducing the canter, proceed with a rising trot on both reins and a few brief canters.

During the 15–20 minute training phase, you focus on movements that improve balance and suppleness. Begin with well-known, simpler exercises and proceed progressively to more challenging or novel activities.

After 5–10 minutes of cooling down with a walk on a loose rein, you conclude your education session. After work, the Horse goes through a crucial phase that should not be shortened because it calms and relaxes the animal.

Give a click with your tongue while nudging your Horse if he refuses to move forward with your assistance. If he doesn't respond, squeeze once more, click your tongue, and tap your leg smartly with your whip directly behind it. Use the whip on your Horse's shoulder if he refuses to accept the touch behind the leg. The assistance must be specific and transient. Avoid repeatedly nudging the Horse with your legs using this "nudge-click-smack" technique; doing so will make him turn off entirely. When your Horse doesn't respond, don't merely gradually apply more pressure with your leg—this will only have a deadening effect. It could be harder to motivate a slow horse to move forward. With certain lethargic horses, strong leg aids, continuous whipping, or even spurs may be effective, but there's a chance the Horse will grow bitter. A diet richer in energy can motivate many lethargic horses to become more proactive.

Viewpoint (Yours)

You must start seriously training your Andalusian Horse when he becomes accustomed to his pasture. That is to say; you can now teach him things on a long lead line or in a circular enclosure with success. We'll go into great detail about this in our next chapters. To help him become acclimated to his surroundings, make sure you stroll with him. To help him overcome his concerns and learn to accept the world as it is, expose him to a wide range of people, horses, and locations. The Andalusian Horse socializes for the whole of its life. You can't keep him in the paddock, never let him interact with people, and then expect him to act normally when he does. It takes a lifetime to socialize and train an Andalusian horse. Daily little steps will make a big difference.

Fear Embracing and Getting Over It

Remember that horses experience periods of fear imprinting. In these stages, phobias may emerge in your Horse. Any unfavorable stimuli have the potential to permanently damage your Horse, giving him lifelong terror.

For instance, if a guy mistreats your Andalusian Horse at this age, he may develop a fear of all men. If a child is constantly tugging on his tail, he may develop a fear of children.

Try not to expose your Andalusian Horse to unpleasant stimuli, such as fireworks or loud noises, yelling in annoyance, or activities that could cause him unnecessary discomfort if you don't want him to become fearful. At no point in his life should you be overly strict with him; instead, be kind. Take him on frequent walks around the stables to expose him to normal environmental stimuli, such as traffic and loud music, to help him overcome his scared attitude and learn that most stimuli are harmless. He will become less fearful as you expose him to the outside world.

Naturally, some horses experience strange phobias. My Horse became fearful when he was left alone in the stables without any other horses to accompany him. Every day, I took him farther and farther. I would force him to go a little farther and stand for five minutes every day before I came back. I kept saying, "Good boy, good boy, good boy," to him each time. After about five minutes, we had moved out enough that he could not see the other horses. We carried on for an hour-long trail ride as he didn't appear to be experiencing any more concerns about it. He never again felt afraid to go out on his own. It took an entire bag of goodies for both of us to get over that one. On the bright side, we did manage to get a good amount of exercise.

For example, as happened to one of my horses, your Andalusian Horse may develop anxiety when crossing a tarp on the grass. I wonder whether he was afraid he would trip, fall, or slip. For whatever reason, he refused to use the tarp as a walkway. This was resolved when he saw that another horse was led over the tarp, and the animal had not suffered any harm. His eyes showed surprise, and his ears sprang straight up. After that, he never felt afraid again since he followed the other horse over the tarp. Always repeatedly tell him, "Good boy," whenever he conquers a fear. Let him understand that he won't be harmed by the things he fears. Assist him in forming constructive associations rather than destructive ones.

Your Andalusian Horse may develop timidity if he has a negative encounter with another person, Horse, or animal. However, if you take the time to help him overcome this fear and recondition him, it need not last forever.

It's good to show him that not everyone is the Unabomber by exposing him to horses, other animals, and nice, joyful people. For obvious reasons, you should avoid someone who yelled at your Andalusian Horse while they were at the stables. Help him get over his phobia of people by exposing him to other calmer, more gentle individuals. A vital component of socializing your Andalusian Horse is helping him overcome his fear.

You might also want to show him other aspects of who you are. You can shave it off and wear a hat if you're an adult male with a beard. In addition, if you so choose (I heard it grows back thicker). Instead of pants or jeans, you can wear a dress, shorts or sunglasses.

You can even switch up your hairstyle, shampoo, and aftershave by using a different scent. He'll be aware of these modifications. He will accept that occasionally, your appearance or aroma changes if you keep talking to him and reassure him that everything is OK when you look different. He won't be as anxious about change after that.

Continue reading to learn how to look after your new best buddy.

Section 5: The Methodologies

You know that horses are incapable of reasoning, which is one of the main challenges in horse training. To know what works and why, you must comprehend how they think.

Their innate dread of pain and punishment, which has been ingrained in them for millennia, is what makes Marco trainable. This dread can be used to teach a horse obedience.

We know the horse's concern, but we must not misuse this understanding since the horse is overly alarmed. It can backfire, and it usually does. If it doesn't work out, you'll run into problems training the horse.

A horse has to learn many things, one of which is to trust you. A horse will never believe in you if you don't believe in yourself. The secret to training horses is these two things.

You may instill confidence in a horse in several ways. This particular one dates back to the 1800s. It's also the simplest method for building your horse's self-confidence.

This confidence plays on horse fear, but it never abuses it. You somehow wisely take advantage of fear to win the horse's trust. It is similar to letting a child watch a scary movie and covering him when he is afraid.

You must be present to reassure the terrified horse that everything is well.

You can pet and converse with him to help him feel less afraid. Speak in a friendly manner. You will essentially be his superhero for the horse, and he will rely on that.

To help you understand what we mean, here is an example. A man and some horseback riders encountered a large stream. Other people's horses will cross the stream, but they have no issue crossing the river.

The rider, distraught, started using his ribs to steer his horse. The poor horse feared the flowing water, yet he still wanted to follow the rider's instructions. The horse began to pace back and forth, smelling the water but not going over it at times. The rider repeatedly kicked the horse's ribs.

Had the rider taken a moment to reflect, he might have realized that the horse was simply afraid and not being disobedient. He must assist the horse. He must speak to the horse and give him comforting strokes.

The horse is only made more fearful of running water by the rider's actions. Not only will he be punished for his fear of rushing water, but he will also keep experiencing it.

Let's now examine it from the perspective of the horse.

You are an unreasonable horse. Your impulse is to protect yourself. Fear governs the ability to survive. You avoid risk because of fear. This terror is what sustains your life.

Let's now adopt a horse-riders perspective. Standing at the brink of a rushing body of water Because you believe there to be some sort of danger there, you dare not cross it. In addition, you get kicked in the ribs by someone on your back who gets angry that you won't go into the water and continue.

You now feel punished in addition to being terrified of flowing water. Your instincts tell you not to, yet you want to follow through. The horse's rider could have talked in a gentle, comforting voice if he had noticed his horse's fear as the animal got closer to the water's edge and understood that it wasn't disobedience that prevented the animal from crossing. To reassure the horse that everything was well, he may have patted it. Even better, he could let the horse investigate and smell the water for himself.

Instead, he is now controlling a terrified, bewildered horse that feels chastised and has less faith in the rider. The story might have ended differently if the motorcyclists had responded differently. Keep in mind that your horses depend on you to be their superhero. Therefore, you must be able to distinguish between being scared and being disobedient.

7. Getting Them Started Early in the Saddle: The Child Rider in Training

Children and horses have been excellent teammates for generations. Taking care of a living creature and demonstrating empathy and understanding for its well-being can help children become more mature and capable of taking on more responsibilities. Finding the ideal pony or horse and, possibly, a teacher is necessary before parents with equestrian experience decide to start their kids riding. But making a judgment about a child who cries out for a pony can be difficult and perplexing for parents who are not familiar with horses.

A lot of parents worry about their children getting hurt badly when riding. Yes, there is a danger—the same risk as letting a kid play baseball or football. But there's also the added risk because the horse is a sentient being with a thought of its own. There are things parents can do to lessen the risk to their kids.

The best action for these parents is to locate a riding school specializing in instruction for young riders. Horses at these establishments are utilized especially for beginning instruction. These horses are usually older, extremely well-trained, and incredibly understanding of a novice child's misbehavior. Additionally, a facility like this frequently hosts summer horseback riding camps, which are excellent for acquainting young riders with the world of horses. Your youngster will create lifelong memories at horse-themed summer camp. Many adult riders can still recall every horse they rode at summer camp when they were nine, even after attending for over thirty years. These kinds of experiences can assist young people in deciding whether riding is something they would like to pursue as a pastime or as a possible sport.

It may take some time to decide which riding discipline your youngster enjoys, so you may need to find out. She might try Western riding (Western saddle with horn) or start with English riding in a tight contact (hunt seat) saddle without a horn.

Since horses are an expensive hobby, the best way to introduce your child to riding is to enroll her in a summer camp for horseback riding (which can be overnight in another state or just a day camp in your area). She should also be outfitted with a riding safety vest, a certified helmet (ASTM/SEI certified), and appropriate footwear (smooth sole, heel jodhpur boots that cover the ankle). Gloves and riding clothes (such as breeches, jodhpurs, or riding jeans) are additional gear she would need. You can get a cheap, approved helmet for less than $100. Similarly, short faux leather boots can be purchased for less than $100. A safety vest will probably set you back more than $100, but you may need to buy it later when your youngster starts to jump or ride at quicker speeds, like the canter or gallop. Gloves must be reasonably priced, ranging from $15 to $22. If your child rides a Western, you can wear regular jeans. She might require jodhpurs, breeches, or riding denim with seams designed to keep the rider's inside leg from rubbing against them if she is riding English.

More expensive options are available for helmets (some as much as $500!) and other gear, but you may buy the less expensive ones now while your child is still learning the sport and developing. If not, it becomes expensive to replace things that she outgrows.

All you need to get your child started riding is a reputable facility with qualified teachers, horses that are suitable for young riders, and appropriate clothing. You will want to save these moments, so don't forget to bring your video camera.

Horses are creatures of prey. They are inherently afraid of being eaten by bears or cougars, and they never know what to do if they spot an elk or deer. Be ready for your horse to respond if you encounter an unusual creature while on the trail. You could be at risk from this. Your Arab can attempt to flip you off his back or make a sudden, high-jumping move that knocks you off balance. I'm only trying to get you ready, not to frighten you. Some Arabs will just stop and evaluate the circumstances. The most desired response is that one.

Gently avert your Arab's face from the threat and walk in that direction if he freezes to evaluate the situation. Keep him from backing away from predators, not even at a trot. The bear or cougar will typically follow the running instinctively. Do not run or let your horse trot. Others will sprint in the other direction, and you could find it hard to keep him under control. It could be necessary for you to leap off or just hold on for a few hundred yards.

While you are building a relationship with your Arab, there are a lot of problems you can have to deal with. You have to get ready ahead of time. He might be your true love if you know the risks and have everything ready beforehand. When riding, we advise you to always use a safety helmet. If you are riding a trail, we advise you to bring a second rider whenever possible.

You'll get out and move more due to this physical activity. Simply put, saying.

Cleaning: Scrubbing

At least four times a week, you should brush your Arab's coat and give his hooves a good cleaning when an Arab sheds in the spring; daily brushing is best. Before the warm summer arrives, he will have to lose his whole winter coat.

It's mutually soothing, I can guarantee you, before the long day starts.

You will have many therapeutic and bonding experiences with your Arab through this. As much as you enjoy brushing him, he will adore being brushed. While you are brushing him, converse with him. Talk to him frequently using his name. Say "good boy" each time he stands up straight. Say "Stand" if he starts to try to get away from you or move about. Say "Good Boy" to him when he stops moving, and then say it repeatedly. Inexperienced Arabs may attempt to bite or kick you. NEVER ALLOW EITHER TO OCCUR! You must take precautions for your safety whenever you are with an Arab. Ensure he's not about to kick you by keeping a close eye on him. He might be considering it if he is standing with one leg bent back. If you never let him, he will never bite or kick you.

You might want to give him some room while you move around him to ensure that he misses his kick if he attempts. You have to smack his nose away and tell him, "No biting," if he attempts to chew on your arm. You only need to backhand lightly. Never hit your Arab very hard if you do. He will never consider biting or kicking you until he fully bonds with you. Brush his entire body, neck, face, and legs if necessary. You'll clean every inch of his body, from the muck to the dust.

Always keep oneself safe. Brush his mane and for-lock with a detangling brush, carefully brushing out all tangles. Some tangles require cutting out because they are so severe. Once the mane is finished, do the same with his tail. Maybe you can stand behind him and brush his tail in the future.

    We advise you to start by standing to one side of his back and softly brushing his tail to one side. Keep in mind that you and your Arab can become close very quickly or very slowly. It is best for everyone when you choose your Arab if he seems devoted to you before making a purchase. That will guarantee that the bonding process happens considerably faster. The bonding process involves all you do at the beginning with your Arab. With your Arab, you are progressively forging a wholesome, long-lasting friendship. Please savor every moment as you go.

Taking a bath

You might need to give your new best friend lots of baths. But remember that his natural oils keep his skin and hair healthy. Washing too much can remove those oils. It is preferable to wash your Arab just once a season, during the warm months. Ensure you purchase a warm-water washing stall and high-quality horse shampoo, such as Mane & Tail Shampoo.

Take your Arab with you into the laundry room.

2. Attach your Arab's Lead Rope to the hitching rail with care now.

3. turn on the water once your Arab is inside the washing machine. Use your fingertips to feel the water's

temperature before soaking your Arab. Make sure the water is lukewarm and pleasant.

4. After thoroughly wetting your Arab's body, massage the shampoo to produce a little foam. Take care not to use so little that you can't get a rich lather or so much that you can't rinse it all out. Try your best to avoid his eyes and mouth. Rinse face when bathing if needed.

5. Tip: Give his head the last wash. This is the bit he would find objectionable.

6. Now rinse him well using lukewarm water.

Using your hands, gently massage the shampoo from top to bottom. Repeat this a few times to remove all of the shampoo so that his natural oils can start working to keep him healthy.

7. Now shut off the water and use a towel to pat him dry. Give him a good massage. Take him to a place where he can dry off in the sun. Remember that right after getting bathed, he will roll in the mud or dirt as soon as possible. It is best to wait until he is dry before allowing that.

paws

When running and walking, your Arab needs to be able to grip with his hooves. You should clean your Arab's hooves whenever you take him out of the stall. You would be familiar with removing dirt, manure, and other debris from the hooves with a hoof pick. It is crucial because tiny gravel fragments might become lodged and hurt your Arab. Cleanse each hoof by picking up each foot separately.

The majority of horses require hoof trims every six to eight weeks. You may hire a farrier to come and trim for you or learn how to do this with a trimmer and file. The trimmer resembles a hybrid of a nail clipper and a set of enormous pliers. The rough file is huge. Most of the time, the hoof can be filed smoothly in a few strokes after reducing it to a ¼ to ½ inch. Avoid cutting the hoof too short, as this may cause bleeding. After clipping, some horse owners choose to always shoe their mount.

Some horses can walk anywhere without shoes because of their extremely strong hooves. Some people find it difficult to walk on jagged pebbles or stones. Strap-on shoes are an additional choice. These can be taken off when not needed and put on when needed. You may choose to wear shoes exclusively on your front two feet. Since Arabs place the majority of their weight on their front foot, this is frequently sufficient.

At the very least, you should have a farrier trim your horse when you initially get it done. Should you want to trim yourself in the future, please take great care with the trimming. Costly are farriers. "You need to start with a large fortune if you want to have a small fortune after owning horses for a few years," it is said. Another proverb goes, "The human brain is the most amazing organ in the human body; it thinks and functions well every day, 365 days a year, from the moment of your birth until you fall in love with a horse." Thus, you might use this to caution about the cost of owning your horse in the long run.

As you read this book, we anticipate it will already be too late. Either you already have feelings for your horse, or you already have feelings for the concept of purchasing your first Arab. In any case, it's probably too late to heed any caution. I have also underlined the potential for risk with Arabs. It is estimated that 100 deaths annually in the United States are related to riding or handling horses; most of these deaths are accidental, and the Arabs did not intend to kill the victim. An estimated 1000–2000 head injuries occur annually, most of which are treated with survival but leave the victim permanently altered. Again, for this reason, we advise you to use a safety helmet when riding.

The Teeth of Your Arab

Horses have teeth designed for grazing.

There are 12 incisors in the front of the mouth of an adult horse.

The premolars and molars are two of the 24 teeth designed for chewing.

"Tushes" are the extra four canine teeth stallions and geldings beneath their incisors.

In front of the molars, some horses—male and female alike—will also acquire one to four tiny vestigial teeth, or "wolf," teeth.

A horse's teeth can be used to determine how old it is.

Throughout life, teeth erupt and become worn down from grazing.

Horses experience variations in the angle at which the chewing surfaces touch, as well as a characteristic wear pattern and tooth form.

Horses' food digestibility is hampered if their teeth lack a flat surface to chew.

Regular dental examinations are a good idea, but no more than once a year is recommended.

Typically, veterinarians advise having your Arab dog's teeth floated every one to four years, ideally by the time the animal is ten.

Filing down all the sharp points and edges to create a level chewing surface is known as "floating" your horse's teeth.

Increased revenue and outlays for your budget!

Eyes: Of all land mammals, horses have the largest eyes.

Horses can see over 350 degrees and have great day and night vision.

Similar to red-green color blindness in humans, horses have partial color blindness.

Your veterinarian should examine your Arab's eyes regularly. Every day, you ought to examine your Arab's eyes. Regular inspection of his stall and paddock is necessary to remove any sharp or pointed objects, such as loose nails or screw tips poking through.

Additionally, search for and remove any loose, sharp wires or splinters. The rationale is that your Arab runs the risk of getting an eye-piercing. During one of your routine observations, you might see that your Arab's eye is almost completely swollen shut. It's likely that your Arab just has a small piece of grass, dust, or dirt in his eye. Try using a medicine called "Vetericyn" Ophthalmic Gel for irritated eyes before calling the veterinarian. After cleaning your hands, apply a thick gel layer to your fingertip and place it slightly above his lower eyelid. He'll undoubtedly want to move away from you but resist the urge to let him touch your hand with his eye. His eye is itching and feels wonderful, so he'll want to do that. This will assist in distributing the gel across his eyeball's surface.

Should the edema not subside after a day, you can choose to schedule a stable appointment with your veterinarian. Even after losing one eye to blindness, some horses can still be ridden and function normally most of the time. Some horses go blind, but if there's no possibility of a stumble, they could be able to be ridden in mild terrain. That would only happen in a lifetime partnership between a strong horse and rider. This book is meant to educate you on how to create, tend to, and grow that lifetime relationship.

The lifespan of a horse is 25 to 30 years. There are Arabs who survive into their 40s and sometimes even older. In the 1800s, a horse was reported to have lived for 62 years. A pony is known to have died in 2007 at age 56. The relationship and affection you share with your Arab will only deepen with each passing year, even though most of it will blossom in the first year. I like to put my chest against my Arab's neck, rub my face against his, and hug him around the base of his neck. I used to do this with him before I bought him to make sure he was a loving Arab that I could get to know.

Examining Your Arabian Vet

Before committing to a new horse, I will always get it checked out by a veterinarian. I usually won't get another checkup for another one to four years or until I start to notice any health issues. I want the veterinarian to weigh and examine his eyes, teeth, and hooves every time they visit. To maintain your Arab's health throughout their life, general care requirements must be met in addition to appropriate feeding and exercise. These consist of regular veterinarian care for teeth, feet, and immunizations; regular grooming and weatherproofing; and management of parasites. A reputable veterinarian will recommend foods and drugs for treatment. Elderly horses (those over 20 years of age) should see their veterinarian at least twice a year, if not more regularly, as sickness is more common and easier to diagnose in older animals.

Your horse's doctor can suggest a wellness program with frequent blood testing. I have owned my three cross-bred Arabs for ten years; they are over twenty years old. My closest friends treat my stables more like a retirement community! Only one of the three can be ridden right now, but I want to give them the best possible life. These are happy horses living in a tiny heaven. They are fortunate.